COLORADO

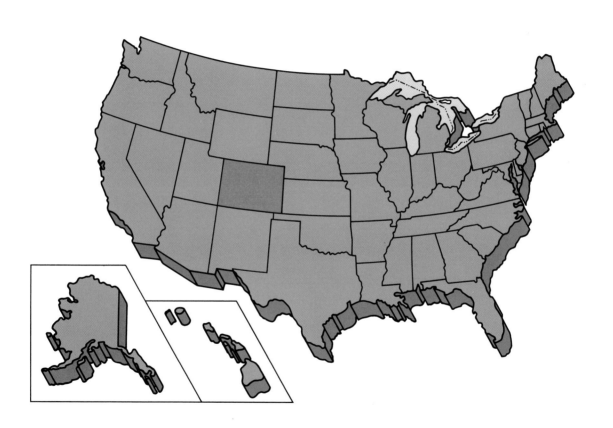

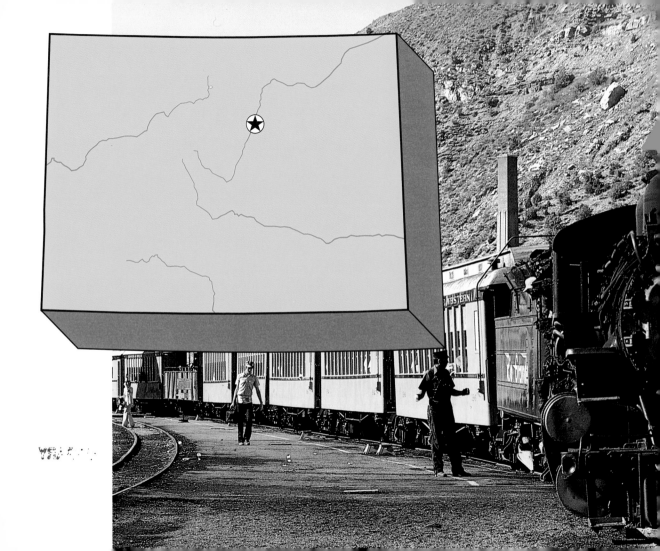

COLORADO

Sara Bledsoe

Lerner Publications Company

LIBRARY OF CONGRESS
CATALOGING-IN-PUBLICATION DATA
Bledsoe, Sara.
    Colorado / Sara Bledsoe.
      p. cm. — (Hello USA)
    Includes index.
    Summary: Introduces the geography, history, people, industries, and environmental concerns of the Rocky Mountain State.
    ISBN 0-8225-2750-2 (lib. bdg.)
    1. Colorado—Juvenile literature.
    [1. Colorado.] I. Title. II. Series.
    F776.3.B58 1993
    978.8—dc20   92-31054
                        CIP
                         AC

Cover photograph by Kent & Donna Dannen.

The glossary that begins on page 68 gives definitions of words shown in **bold type** in the text.

CONTENTS

Royal Gorge

Did You Know . . . ?

☐ The highest suspension bridge in the world spans the Royal Gorge, a canyon along the Arkansas River in central Colorado. The river lies 1,053 feet (321 meters) below the bridge.

☐ Boulder, Colorado, is the only U.S. city that gets its water from the melting ice of a glacier. The Arapahoe Glacier, which fills a high mountain valley just northwest of Boulder, supplies the city.

❑ Parts of Colorado's Great Plains region receive more hail than any other area in North America.

❑ In 1893 Denver, Colorado, became the first major city in the world to grant women the right to vote.

❑ The state of Colorado takes its name from the Colorado River. Because the river flows through canyons of red stone, early Spanish explorers named the waterway *Colorado,* which means "colored red."

A Trip Around the State

Colorado's claim to fame is not that it's the biggest, the smallest, or even the most populated state in the nation. Colorado, sometimes called the Roof of North America, is the tallest state!

With more than 50 peaks reaching above 14,000 feet (4,270 m), Colorado can boast about having the highest mountains in the United States. These rugged peaks are part of the Rocky Mountains, a long chain of mountains that runs north to south from Canada to New Mexico.

Colorado, a Rocky Mountain state, is bordered by New Mexico, Arizona, Utah, Wyoming, Nebraska, Kansas, and Oklahoma. The Rocky Mountains (also called the Rockies) are probably the best-known feature of Colorado. But the Rocky Mountain region, which covers central Colorado, makes up only about two-fifths of the state. The Great Plains region, which lies east of the Rockies, stretches across another two-fifths of Colorado. The Colorado Plateau covers the remaining one-fifth of the state.

At 14,433 feet (4,399 meters), Mount Elbert pierces the sky near Leadville, Colorado. It is the highest peak in the entire Rocky Mountain system.

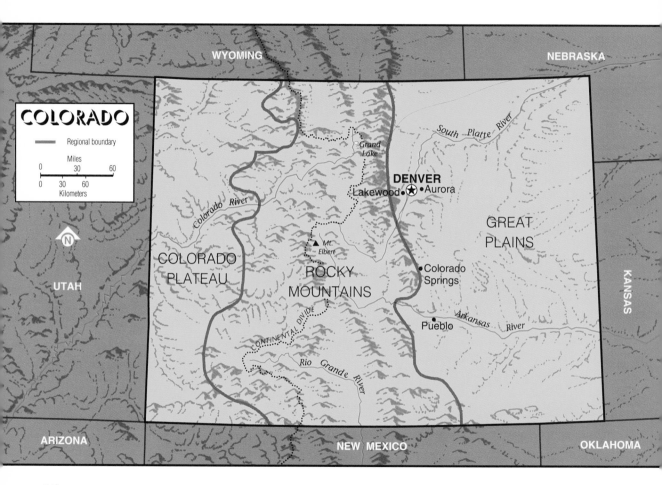

COLORADO

Regional boundary

Miles
0   30   60

0   30   60
Kilometers

N

WYOMING

NEBRASKA

UTAH

KANSAS

ARIZONA

NEW MEXICO

OKLAHOMA

COLORADO
PLATEAU

ROCKY
MOUNTAINS

GREAT
PLAINS

Grand
Lake

DENVER
Lakewood • ★ • Aurora

Colorado River

South Platte River

Mt.
Elbert

Colorado
Springs

Pueblo

Arkansas River

Rio Grande River

CONTINENTAL DIVIDE

Colorado's Rockies are made up of five mountain ranges. Four **parks,** or high and wide valleys, separate the ranges. The Front Range is the first row of mountains to rise up from the Great Plains in north central Colorado.

Workers have built highways through many of the mountain **passes,** or openings low in the ranges. The highways have made it easy for people to travel from one part of the state to another, except when the passes are closed because of a severe snowstorm or the threat of an avalanche.

The **Continental Divide** runs along the tops of the Rocky Mountains. The divide separates Colorado's Rockies into sections known as the Eastern Slope and the

A hiker crosses the Continental Divide in Colorado's Rocky Mountain National Park.

Western Slope. Rivers that begin on the Eastern Slope flow toward the Atlantic Ocean. Rivers on the Western Slope flow toward the Pacific Ocean.

11

Strong winds often cut across Colorado's open plains, leaving ridge marks in the snow.

Colorado's Great Plains region is part of a vast stretch of flat land that extends from Canada to Texas. Low hills and **bluffs**, or cliffs, occasionally break the land. At the western edge of the plains, a narrow strip at the foot of the Front Range is home to more than 80 percent of Colorado's population. Most of Colorado's farms and ranches are located on the rest of the Great Plains region, much of which is covered with grasses.

Like other **plateaus**, the Colorado Plateau region looks like a high tabletop. It is very hard and rocky. Over thousands of years, rivers rushing down from the mountains have worn through some of the rock, making deep valleys. The rivers have also created **mesas**, or steep-sided hills with flat tops. Throughout the region, gusting winds have carved out huge rock formations that look big enough to have been made by giants.

At the Colorado National Monument, on the Colorado Plateau, jagged rock formations jut up from the ground.

13

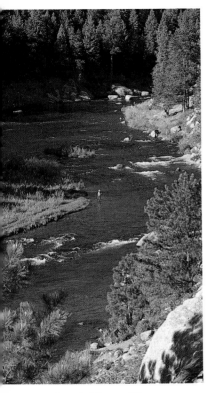

South Platte River

Several major rivers flow across Colorado. High in the mountains, the Colorado River begins its westward journey at Grand Lake. The Rio Grande (Spanish for "big river") starts its course in southern Colorado. The South Platte and the Arkansas rivers race down the Eastern Slope, then flow across the plains.

Coloradans experience all four seasons. But Colorado's weather is unusual because it can change dramatically within short distances. Just 90 miles (145 kilometers) from a snowstorm in the mountains, for instance, the winter sun might be warming the plains.

January temperatures average 28° F (−2° C) on the Great Plains and 18° F (−8° C) in the mountains. Snowstorms are common in the winter—especially in the mountains, where up to 400 inches (1,016 centimeters) a year may fall. But a snowstorm one day is likely to be followed by bright sunshine the next. In fact, Colorado has about 300 days of sunshine a year.

Snow (above left) **and rain** (above center) **bring colorful wildflowers, such as the wild iris** (above right), **in the spring.**

Summers can be hot, windy, and dusty on the plains. Sometimes, temperatures reach 100° F (38° C), causing many Coloradans to head for the mountains. The plains may not receive rain for weeks in the summer. But, like clockwork, thunderstorms develop in the mountains almost every afternoon between the hours of four and six.

15

A great variety of animals and plants thrive in Colorado. Antelope, kit foxes, ground squirrels, badgers, coyotes, jackrabbits, and several types of snakes—including rattlesnakes—live on the Great Plains. More than 100 different kinds of plants grow on the region's native sod, or grassland. These plants include buffalo grass, wildflowers, cottonwood and yucca trees, and prickly pear cactuses.

Ponderosa pines and cedar trees grow on the foothills of the mountains. Trees such as aspen, spruce, and fir grow higher up in the mountains. Mule deer, moose, elks, mountain lions, black bears, and bighorn sheep are also found on the slopes. In northwestern Colorado, wild horses roam the plateau.

An elk nibbles on the twigs and needles of a frozen tree branch.

Coyote *(top left)*
Pine tree *(top right)*
Scarlet paintbrush *(left)*

17

A huge dinosaur footprint *(left)* found in one of Colorado's coal mines is at least 60 million years old. The Rocky Mountain columbine *(inset)* is Colorado's state flower.

Colorado's Story

Thousands of years before Colorado became a state, Native Americans lived on the mountains, mesas, and plains in the area. Skeletons and a few other remains are about the only evidence we have of these ancient people, and so we know very little about how they lived.

Yucca

Pottery, jewelry, and tools made by later Indians—the Anasazi—have also been discovered in Colorado. The Anasazi, who lived on the Colorado Plateau from about 100 B.C. to A.D. 1300, hunted and planted gardens for food. They wove baskets using straw, vines, rushes, and the sharp, pointed leaves of the yucca plant. Because of this skill, the Anasazi are also known as the Basket Makers.

Around the year 750, the Anasazi began to construct apartment-like buildings that we now call *pueblos*, the Spanish word for "towns." To build the pueblos, the Indians made bricks from clay. Each pueblo had several floors connected by ladders.

Cliff Palace, the largest cliff dwelling at Mesa Verde National Park, contains hundreds of rooms.

The Anasazi Indians dug canals to channel water to their crops.

Later, the Anasazi built their homes into the sides of cliffs and eventually became known as Cliff Dwellers. Cliff dwellings shielded the Indians from their enemies and from harsh weather.

The Anasazi were creative farm-ers, too. To water their crops, the Indians dug narrow ditches from rivers and lakes to their gardens. This method, called **irrigation,** allowed water to flow through the channels to keep the crops healthy during the dry summers.

In the year 1276, a long **drought** began. No snow, hail, or rain fell in any large amount for about 23 years. The Anasazi abandoned their dying crops and moved farther south.

Around 1500 the Bannock and the Ute Indians journeyed on foot from what is now Utah to Colorado's Western Slope. At the same time, the Apache, Comanche, Kiowa, Navajo, and Pawnee were living in southern Colorado. Later, Arapaho and Cheyenne Indians settled on Colorado's plains.

In 1521, south of Colorado in what is now Mexico, Spanish soldiers set up a **colony,** or settlement, on Indian lands. The colony, called New Spain, and its Indians were ruled by faraway Spain.

Spanish explorers saw this deep canyon for the first time in 1540. They named the river at the bottom the Colorado.

The Arapaho were some of the first Indians to trade with the Spaniards on the Great Plains.

The Spaniards also tried to control the Indians in what is now Colorado, but the Indians defeated the Spanish forces. The Indians were more than willing, however, to trade with the Spaniards. By the late 1600s, Spanish traders were driving mule trains from Santa Fe, New Mexico, over the Rockies to Indian settlements along the Arkansas River. Later, this route became part of the Santa Fe Trail, which extended to Missouri.

The Spaniards traded goods such as whiskey, rifles, steel needles, and iron pots for furs and hides provided by the Indians. The Spaniards then sold the furs and hides in Europe, making huge profits.

In 1682 René-Robert Cavelier de La Salle, a French explorer, claimed a huge chunk of land in central North America for France. He called the region Louisiana. La Salle's Louisiana included what is now eastern Colorado.

Members of the Pike expedition *(below)* thought that Pikes Peak *(left)* was too high to climb. Nowadays, thousands of people take a cog railroad to the top each year.

When a Spaniard named Juan de Ulibari rode across the Rocky Mountains for the first time in 1706, he discovered that the Indians in eastern Colorado had gotten various items from the French. To protect Spanish trade with the Indians, Ulibari promptly claimed what is now Colorado for Spain. Both France and Spain claimed they owned eastern Colorado at the same time!

In the early 1800s, the two countries agreed that France controlled all of Louisiana. But France was involved in a costly war with Great Britain and needed money. To help pay for the war, France sold Louisiana to the United States in 1803. This sale, called the Louisiana Purchase, doubled the size of the United States.

The U.S. government hired an expedition to explore part of the recently purchased land. In 1806 Zebulon Pike, a young army lieutenant, led the expedition to the Rocky Mountains in Colorado.

While crossing the Great Plains, Pike saw a majestic peak a hundred miles away. This mountain would later be named Pikes Peak—now one of the best-known landmarks in the United States. Pike then ventured over the Rockies into Spanish territory, where he was captured by Spaniards and jailed for one year before being released.

In 1821 New Spain gained its independence from Spain and became the country of Mexico. Mexico took over the territories Spain had claimed, including what is now western Colorado. Many **Anglos**, or people from the United States, moved to the Mexican territories to trade with the people there.

Mexico and the United States disagreed about where the border between the two countries actually lay. To solve the dispute, the United States wanted to buy some of Mexico's territories. When Mexico refused to hear the terms, the United States sent troops across the border, starting the Mexican War (1846–1848). Mexico was easily defeated.

The Ute perform the bear dance, an annual ceremony to welcome spring.

After the war, Mexico was forced to give what are now California, Nevada, Utah, and parts of Arizona, New Mexico, Wyoming, and Colorado to the United States. More Anglos moved to the new U.S. territory, building settlements on the homelands of the Indians.

The U.S. government signed **treaties,** or written agreements, with the Indians in the area. The treaties granted the Indians large tracts of land, called **reservations,** on which they were to live undisturbed by Anglo settlers. But before long, trappers and traders broke the treaties by settling on the outskirts of the reservations.

In 1858 gold was discovered in mountain streams along the Front Range, triggering the Pikes Peak gold rush. Nearly 50,000 people flooded the area with high hopes of making a fortune. They set up tents or made makeshift homes. A few gold prospectors became rich by panning for gold, but many people did not find any gold at all, and some nearly starved.

Besides the prospectors, thousands of men and women came with other dreams of how to get rich. They sold food, clothing, whiskey, donkeys, mining equipment,

28

and other supplies to the miners at high prices.

These businesspeople also built hotels, stores, saloons, stables, houses, churches, and schools. In 1860 the city of Denver was established near the gold mines along the Front Range.

Before long, not much gold was left to be mined, and the boom came to an end. People left Colorado by the thousands, but the U.S. government wanted them to stay. It forced the Indians to sell large chunks of reservation land. Every interested Anglo family was given 160 acres (65 hectares) of the former reservation land for free, as long as the family used it for farming or planting trees.

Denver, founded in 1860, quickly became the center of activity along the Front Range.

The Sand Creek Massacre

As cattle ranchers settled on the Great Plains in Colorado in the early 1860s, life changed quickly for the plains Indians. The large herds of livestock ate so much grass that there was little left for the Indians' horses. And many of the new settlers took pleasure in hunting wild buffalo purely for sport. The Arapaho and Cheyenne Indians depended on buffalo for food and many other needs. As the buffalo herds dwindled, the Indians grew angry.

Tensions rose between the Indians and the settlers, and so did violence. Some bands of Indians attacked wagon trains. And U.S. soldiers killed peaceful Indians. Cheyenne leader Black Kettle wanted to keep peace, and the U.S. Army promised him and his people protection from attacks as long as they camped at

Fort Lyon. There, Black Kettle and some other Cheyenne were told to move north to Sand Creek, where they would still be safe.

But Colorado's governor had called together a volunteer army regiment to protect settlers from Indians. To prove the need for the regiment, the governor had to use it. So in 1864 he ordered 700 troops, led by Colonel John Chivington, to march to Sand Creek.

At dawn, Chivington commanded his men to attack the sleeping village. As the Cheyenne stumbled out of their lodges, they tried to fight or hide. Two hundred or more were killed. More than half were women and children. The surprise attack became known as the Sand Creek Massacre.

In 1876 the United States celebrated its centennial anniversary, an event honoring the country's 100th birthday. That same year, Colorado joined the Union as the 38th state and was nicknamed the Centennial State. Denver became the state capital.

The red "C" on Colorado's state flag stands for more than the name of the state. It also refers to the reddish Colorado River and to the "red people"—the Indians. The gold circle in the center symbolizes Colorado's mineral wealth. The state's blue skies and snowcapped mountains are represented by the flag's horizontal blue and white stripes.

In 1878 silver was discovered near Leadville, Colorado, and the state experienced another mining boom. Prospectors flocked to Colorado's western mountains, which belonged to the Ute Indians. Land-hungry Anglos flooded into the mountains to build homes. The Ute's reservations were becoming smaller and smaller.

While more people were moving west to mine or to get free land, transportation was improving. The U.S. government gave railroad companies free land on which to build train tracks so that gold, silver, and people could be easily transported to and from Colorado. Later, the railroad companies sold trackside land to settlers, making huge profits.

A gold strike near Cripple Creek in 1893 and a growing coal-mining industry kept miners busy for the rest of the 1800s. As more people made Colorado their home, local farmers and ranchers began to make a good living by supplying potatoes, corn, wheat, and beef to Coloradans. The state no longer relied on shipments of food from other places. By 1910 more Coloradans were working on farms and ranches than in mines.

Construction of Colorado's railroads began in the late 1800s.

Miners *(above)* sometimes panned for gold in mountain streams. By the early 1900s, rather than hope for a lucky strike in a gold or silver mine, many Coloradans turned to the more steady job of farming *(right)*.

Silver King and Baby Doe

In the late 1870s, a boom in silver mining made Horace A. W. Tabor a very wealthy man. Tabor —known as the Silver King—and his wife, the beautiful Baby Doe, became a symbol of Colorado's mining booms and busts.

With the profits from his Matchless Mine near Leadville, Horace Tabor spent a lot of money buying expensive gifts and building fancy opera halls. But in 1893, a crash in the price of silver made the Tabors' mine worthless. The Tabors were broke.

Without money from the silver mine, the Tabors counted every penny. But before Horace Tabor died in 1899, he told his wife to watch over the mine, assuring her that someday it would make her rich again.

Baby Doe Tabor followed her husband's instructions. For years she lived alone in poverty, in a wooden shack at the mine's entrance. In 1935 Mrs. Tabor was found—frozen to death—in the shack. Her Matchless Mine never did produce another fortune.

In the early 1900s, miners in Colorado began to depend on another mineral—oil. Large reserves of oil had been discovered in various parts of Colorado, and oil soon replaced gold and silver as the state's most important mineral.

At the same time, the nation was growing dependent on the automobile. Americans wanted to use their cars to see the country. Thousands of vacationers filled their gas tanks with gasoline, some of which had been made from oil drilled in Colorado. Then they headed for the state to view the magnificent scenery.

During World War I (1914–1918), Colorado's farmers grew tons of wheat to help feed U.S. soldiers. During the war, wheat sold for high prices, so farmers took out loans to buy more farmland. When the war ended, the price of wheat fell. Farmers began losing a lot of money on their crops and were unable to pay back their loans.

Oil wells, such as this one in Vineland, Colorado, popped up all over Colorado in the 1920s.

Colorado lost tons of soil during the dust storms of the mid-1930s.

Colorado's economic troubles grew worse in 1929. That year marked the beginning of the Great Depression, a major slump in the U.S. economy that lasted through the 1930s. Businesses closed down, and many men and women couldn't find new jobs. Agriculture was hurting too. For example, the price of a cow dropped from $100 to $16.

Bad weather during the depression added to the farmers' problems. High winds and low rainfall caused blinding dust storms that carried away the rich topsoil of the Great Plains. Some of it blew clear to Washington, D.C.! Crops failed, and thousands of people suffered from lung diseases caused by breathing in the dust-filled air.

During World War II, the U.S. government mined uranium on the Colorado Plateau. The metal was then refined at this plant in Grand Junction, Colorado, and used to produce the highly destructive atomic bomb.

By the early 1940s, during World War II, thousands of new jobs pulled Colorado out of the depression. This time, the state's boom was in manufacturing. Factory workers made guns, bombs, bullets, and planes for the war effort. In addition, the U.S. government moved many of its office workers from Washington, D.C., to Colorado. Denver soon became known as the Nation's Western Capital.

Colorado did not become a world-famous ski resort until the 1960s, but the state's first towrope was installed at Grand Junction in the late 1930s.

News of more government job openings in the 1950s brought thousands of people to the state. With so many more people, the state needed additional supplies of water. The government planned several irrigation projects. Work on the Frying Pan-Arkansas Project, for example, began in the 1960s. The project now channels water from western Colorado to the dry eastern plains.

Another economic boom came to Colorado in the 1970s and early 1980s, when the state began to drill for more oil. Prices for oil were high at the time, and oil companies in the state made a lot of money.

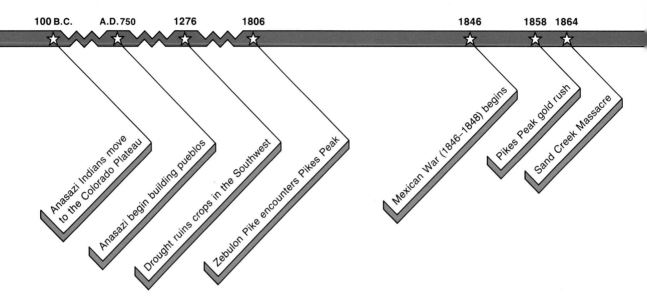

100 B.C.	A.D. 750	1276	1806	1846	1858	1864

Anasazi Indians move to the Colorado Plateau

Anasazi begin building pueblos

Drought ruins crops in the Southwest

Zebulon Pike encounters Pikes Peak

Mexican War (1846–1848) begins

Pikes Peak gold rush

Sand Creek Massacre

By 1983, 16 skyscrapers had been built in Denver with money earned from oil. But the price of oil dropped in the mid-1980s, ending another boom.

Coloradans do not want to repeat history. They are trying instead to avoid booms and busts by creating jobs that will be needed for years to come.

1876 — Colorado becomes the 38th state

1929 — Great Depression begins

1972 — Frying Pan-Arkansas Project begins operations

1993 — Denver International Airport opens

The Denver International Airport, which opened in 1993, has added 4,000 jobs to the Denver area.

41

Living and Working in Colorado

Colorado has changed a lot since the Anasazi first built their pueblos and the miners their temporary one-room shacks. Many more people live in the state nowadays. Between 1970 and 1980, for example, Colorado's population increased by 31 percent, as people moved to the state seeking jobs. In 1990 Colorado's total population was 3.3 million and growing.

Colorado's largest cities are Denver—the capital—Colorado Springs, Aurora, Lakewood, and Pueblo.

All of these cities are located on a narrow strip of land along the eastern edge of the Front Range, which offers some of the most beautiful scenery in the United States. More than 80 percent of Colorado's population, or 2.6 million people, live along this strip.

A resort in Glenwood Springs, Colorado, features a pool fed by hot springwater.

Eighty-three percent of Coloradans are Anglos. Anglos include people whose ancestors came from Great Britain, Russia, Italy, and Germany. **Latinos,** people who either came from or have ancestors from Latin America, are the state's largest minority group. They make up about 13 percent of Colorado's population.

African Americans make up 3 percent of the population. Many are descendants of black families

A Native American boy dances at a powwow, or ceremonial get-together, in Chipita Park, Colorado.

who moved to Colorado in the late 1800s. In the 1970s, many people from Vietnam came to the United States to escape war in their homeland. Many of these **immigrants** settled in Colorado. About 1 percent of Colorado's people are Asian American.

Less than 1 percent of Coloradans are Native American. Some Indians live on the Ute Mountain Ute or the Southern Ute reservations in southwestern Colorado.

At one time, almost every man in Colorado worked in one of the state's mines. Nowadays, only about 1 percent of the state's work force have jobs in mining. Miners and engineers still look for gold

Oil wells dot Colorado's Great Plains region.

and silver. But coal, natural gas, and oil are the state's chief mineral products.

Miners operate huge cranes to dig coal out of the ground. The coal is then shipped in railroad cars to other states, where it is burned as fuel to generate energy for heating and electricity. Natural gas, another source of energy, is sent to other states through underground pipes. Drilling for oil has continued off and on in various parts of the state since the early 1860s.

Ranchers and farmers make up just under 4 percent of Colorado's work force. Throughout the state, ranchers raise beef cattle. Beef is Colorado's most important agricultural product. Sheep, which are raised for their wool and meat, are

Pumpkins are stacked up to be sold at the farmers' market in Boulder.

herded mainly in the mountains. Farmers on the Great Plains grow wheat, corn, and sugar beets. Cantaloupes and tomatoes are grown along the Arkansas River. On the Colorado Plateau, farmers harvest peaches, apples, and grapes.

47

Most of Colorado's cattle graze on the grasses that grow on the Great Plains *(above)*. Each spring and fall the animals are rounded up *(right)*. The calves are branded in spring and weaned and sold in fall. Some ranchers also raise goats *(upper right)*.

Thirteen percent of Colorado's workers make their living by manufacturing products. Many women and men in Colorado work in factories making computers, medical instruments, cars, planes, skiwear, beer, and suitcases. Colorado's manufactured goods are sold in stores throughout the country.

The largest number—78 percent —of Colorado's workers make their living by providing a wide variety of services. People with service jobs include nurses, pilots, bankers, and teachers.

Forest fires sometimes threaten Colorado's wilderness areas. The services of fire fighters are needed to smother the blazes.

Students at the U.S. Air Force Academy learn to navigate a military jet.

Most of the state's service workers hold government jobs. These people make coins, maintain national parks and forests, and serve in the military. The U.S. government has five military bases in Colorado, as well as the U.S. Air Force Academy, where soldiers are trained to be officers.

Tourism also provides service jobs. Close to 28 million people visit Colorado each year for business or pleasure. Service workers sell food, lodging, equipment, and tours to the visitors.

During the winter, vacationers come to Colorado to glide down any of the state's 30 powdery ski slopes. Two of the country's most famous ski resorts are Aspen and Vail, which are open year-round. In the summer, the resorts host conventions. Mountain climbers also come in the summer to scale the highest peaks of the Rockies.

Both tourists and residents delight in Colorado's outdoor wonders. Dinosaur National Monu-

Hikers in Colorado's Rocky Mountains must be prepared for unexpected snowstorms.

ment, Colorado Petrified Forest, Garden of the Gods, and Rocky Mountain National Park are enchanting places to visit. Ancient Anasazi cliff dwellings can be explored at Mesa Verde National Park in southwestern Colorado. In Denver, Elitch Gardens and Lakeside amusement parks offer thrilling rides.

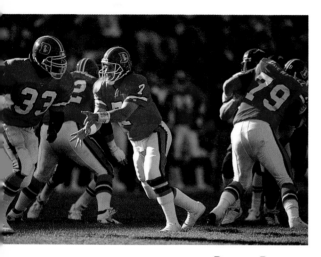

Denver Broncos

Coloradans enjoy watching professional sports. The Denver Broncos play football at Mile High Stadium, and the Denver Nuggets shoot baskets at McNichols Sports Arena. In 1993 Coloradans began cheering on the Colorado Rockies, the state's new major-league baseball team. Colorado State University, the University of Colorado, and the U.S. Air Force Academy also have popular sports teams.

Almost every county in Colorado has a fair and a rodeo. The biggest fair of all, the Colorado State Fair, is held in August and September in Pueblo. Hundreds of people compete for prizes in art, baking, and agriculture. Thousands of visitors enjoy the displays, carnival rides, horse races, rodeos, and musical performances.

December and January are special months in Colorado. The Denver City and County Building celebrates the holidays with one of the largest displays of Christmas lights in the nation.

On New Year's Eve in Colorado, the AdAmAn Club (which adds one new member a year) climbs Pikes Peak. At the stroke of midnight, the members set off fireworks, which can be seen on the plains up to 90 miles (145 km) away. And in mid-January, the National Western Stock Show, complete with professional rodeos, puts on the largest cattle show in the world.

Protecting the Environment

Most Coloradans live in the crowded cities along the Front Range, from Fort Collins in the north to Colorado Springs and Pueblo in the south. The cities and towns along this strip continue to grow. With so many people living and working close together, the Front Range has developed some serious environmental problems. One noticeable problem is **smog**—a dark, heavy haze in the air.

The smoke that pours out of factory smokestacks combines with fog to create smog.

On some days, a thick smog known as the Brown Cloud hangs over the city of Denver. People with asthma and other lung problems have a hard time breathing on these days and are advised to stay inside. In addition, the smog smells bad, and the beautiful Rocky Mountains are hidden behind the brown haze.

The word *smog* is actually a blend of two words—"smoke" and "fog." Fog, a thick mist, occurs naturally. But when fog combines with the chemical-filled smoke that pours out of smokestacks at power plants and factories, smog forms.

The exhaust from cars and other vehicles on Denver's crowded highways contributes to the Brown Cloud.

Factories are responsible for part of the Brown Cloud, but almost half of Denver's smog comes from cars, trucks, buses, and planes operating along the Front Range. When these vehicles burn fuel, they release hydrocarbons and nitrogen oxides—chemicals that cling to fog and form smog.

The Rocky Mountains worsen Denver's smog problem by acting as a barrier, trapping smog in the area. As more people move to the Front Range, increasing the number of motor vehicles in the region, Denver's Brown Cloud may spread to nearby cities.

Airplane traffic over the Front Range has increased since the Denver International Airport opened in 1993.

When the Denver International Airport opened in 1993, more planes began flying over the Front Range. The new airport has turned Denver into a major stopover between the East and West coasts.

As a result, people in the Rocky Mountain region have more flights to choose from. The airport has also added jobs, but some people argue that the airplanes have simply added to the smog problem.

Each person in Colorado can help prevent more smog from forming by using motor vehicles less often, an effort which would reduce the amount of chemicals released into the air. To cut down on trips to the mall, people can call ahead to find out if a store carries the product they are looking for. And customers can walk inside fast-food restaurants instead of letting their car engines run while waiting in drive-through lines.

Businesses can prompt employees to share rides to work by offering reduced parking fees for carpoolers. Employers can also sell bus passes at a discount to encourage their workers to take the bus. And, rather than driving or flying to meetings, workers can communicate with customers in other cities by telephone or computer whenever possible.

Buses can carry many people at one time, reducing the number of vehicles on the road and the amount of exhaust in the air.

In the near future, all of Colorado's drivers may be able to use cleaner-burning fuels such as natural gas or ethanol (a gasoline made from corn), which are currently available at some gas stations. When burned, these forms of energy release fewer chemicals than gasoline does.

Emissions testing helped Denver win an award in 1990 for improving its air quality more than any other U.S. city. But many more changes need to be made before the Brown Cloud can disappear. Everyone enjoys breathing good, clean air. Coloradans can preserve and improve their air quality by doing simple activities on a daily basis.

The state government can help by building more walkways and bikeways, so people will have a safe place to walk, roller-skate, or bicycle to their destinations. And residents in the Denver area can urge the city to set aside money for rapid transit. Rapid transit systems transport large numbers of people using electric trains, which don't pollute the air as much.

In the meantime, Colorado has required drivers to run their cars through an emissions test every year to see how many hydrocarbons and nitrogen oxides they release. Cars that create too much pollution must be properly tuned up before they can be on the road again legally.

Using bike paths can be
both practical and
enjoyable.

Colorado's Famous People

ACTORS

Lon Chaney, Sr. (1883–1930), from Colorado Springs, starred in classic horror films, including *The Hunchback of Notre Dame* and *The Phantom of the Opera*. Because the actor wore a lot of makeup to change his appearance for each new role, he became known as the Man of a Thousand Faces.

Douglas Fairbanks, Sr. (1883–1939), starred in many adventure movies in the 1920s. Two of his most famous films are *The Three Musketeers* and *Robin Hood*. Fairbanks, who grew up in Denver, cofounded the United Artists film studio in 1919.

Antoinette Perry (1888–1946), nicknamed Tony, was a well-known actress and theater director of the early 1900s. The Tony Award, given each year to recognize talented actors in theater, is named after her. Perry was born in Denver.

▲ LON CHANEY, SR.

▲ ANTOINETTE PERRY

◄ DOUGLAS FAIRBANKS, SR.

EARL
▼ CLARK

ATHLETES

Earl ("Dutch") Clark (1906–1978) was a football player from Fowler, Colorado. As a quarterback, Clark led the National Football League in scoring for three seasons and became one of the first members of the National Football Hall of Fame.

Jack Dempsey (1895–1983), considered one of the best boxers of all time, grew up in Manassa, Colorado. Nicknamed the Manassa Mauler, Dempsey held the title for the heavyweight boxing champion for 16 years.

◄ JACK DEMPSEY

Adolph Coors (1847–1919) moved from Germany to Golden, Colorado, and opened the Adolph Coors Company in 1880. The company has grown to be the largest beer maker in Colorado.

David Packard (born 1912), along with William Hewlett, founded the Hewlett-Packard Company in 1939. The partners invented and sold machinery, including equipment for bowling alleys. The company now makes high-tech computers. Packard grew up in Pueblo, Colorado.

◀ ADOLPH COORS

DAVID PACKARD *(right)* ▼

GUIDES

Christopher ("Kit") Carson (1809–1868) was a trapper, trader, guide, and Indian scout in Colorado and other western territories. Carson was known for his ability to find his way along Rocky Mountain trails. In 1838 he operated a trading post in what is now Kit Carson, Colorado.

Ouray (1834–1880), a Ute Indian leader, was widely respected for his skill in settling disputes between white settlers and Indians. He kept peace between settlers and his people for many years. A county, a city, and a mountain in Colorado are all named after him.

◀ KIT CARSON

▲ OURAY

JOURNALIST & PHOTOGRAPHER

Terry Drinkwater (born 1936), from Denver, has been a news reporter for CBS since 1964. His reports have covered many important events, such as presidential elections and space voyages.

Laura Gilpin (1891–1979) was a photographer and writer from Colorado Springs. She is best known for her photos of Navajo Indians.

◀ **LAURA GILPIN**

MINING STARS

Margaret ("Molly") Brown (1867–1932) came from a poor family in Missouri before heading for Leadville, Colorado, where she met her husband, J. J. Brown, and made a fortune mining silver. In 1912 Molly sailed on the *Titanic*, a ship thought to be unsinkable. When the boat sank, she helped a lifeboat full of people survive the famous wreck. A play and a movie, both entitled *The Unsinkable Molly Brown*, tell the story of Molly's life.

◀ **MARGARET BROWN**

Carrie Jane Everson (1842–1914) moved from Chicago to Denver, where she became interested in mining practices in the 1870s. In her experiments with ground-up gold ore, she discovered a way to separate the precious metal from its ore. But it wasn't until after her death that she received credit for her accomplishment, called oil flotation, which eventually became a common method for separating metal from ore.

POLITICAL LEADERS

Federico Peña (born 1947) was Denver's mayor from 1983 to 1991. Peña, a Mexican American, served two terms in a city where the population is mostly Anglo. In 1993 U.S. President Clinton named Peña to head the U.S. Department of Transportation.

FEDERICO ▶ PEÑA

Byron R. White (born 1917) was an associate justice of the U.S. Supreme Court from 1962 to 1993. White graduated in 1938

64

from the University of Colorado, where he earned the nickname Whizzer for his skills on the football field. White is from Fort Collins, Colorado.

SCIENTISTS

Scott Carpenter (born 1925), from Boulder, Colorado, was one of the first U.S. astronauts in outer space. In 1962 Carpenter and six other Americans orbited the earth three times in the spacecraft *Mercury*.

Justina Ford (1871–1952), the first African American woman in Colorado to become a doctor, settled in Denver in 1902. During her 50-year career, she delivered at least 7,000 babies in the Denver area, mostly for poor women. Her Denver residence now houses the Black American West Museum and Heritage Center.

▲ BYRON WHITE

SCOTT ► CARPENTER

FLORENCE ► SABIN

◄ JUSTINA FORD

Florence Sabin (1871–1953), of Central City, Colorado, received many honors for her research on tuberculosis, a deadly disease that affects the lungs. In the 1930s, the world-famous doctor tested people in the Denver area for tuberculosis, greatly reducing the number of deaths caused by the disease.

WRITERS

Mary Letha Elting (born 1906), from Creede, Colorado, has written several children's books, including *Wheels and Noises* and *The Answer Book*.

Eugene Field (1850–1895) was an editor of the *Denver Tribune* in the early 1880s. Field, who is best known for his children's poems, wrote *Little Boy Blue* and *Wynken, Blynken and Nod*.

Facts-at-a-Glance

Nickname: Centennial State
Song: "Where the Columbines Grow"
Motto: *Nil sine Numine*
  (Nothing without Providence)
Flower: Rocky Mountain columbine
Tree: blue spruce
Bird: lark bunting

Population: 3,294,394*
Rank in population, nationwide: 26th
Area: 104,100 sq mi (269,619 sq km)
Rank in area, nationwide: 8th
Date and ranking of statehood:
  August 1, 1876, the 38th state
Capital: Denver
Major cities (and populations*):
  Denver (467,610), Colorado Springs (281,140),
  Aurora (222,103), Lakewood (126,481), Pueblo
  (98,640)
U.S. senators: 2
U.S. representatives: 6
Electoral votes: 8

Places to visit: Dinosaur National Monument near Rangely, Buffalo Bill's Grave near Golden, Museum of Western Art in Denver, Durango & Silverton Narrow Gauge Railroad through the San Juan Mountains, U.S. Mint in Denver

Annual events: National Western Stock Show in Denver (Jan.), World Cup Ski Racing Competitions in Vail and Aspen (Feb./March), Ute Mountain Bear Dance in Towaoc (June), Festival of the Arts in Crested Butte (Aug.), Dog Sled Racing in Leadville (Dec.)

*1990 census

66

Natural resources: fertile soil, coal, gold, natural gas, oil, gravel, sand, and stone

Agricultural products: beef, lamb, milk, hay, wheat, corn, beans, potatoes, sugar beets

Manufactured goods: medical instruments, beer, animal feed, computers, newspapers, electrical equipment, luggage, sporting goods

ENDANGERED SPECIES
Mammals—black-footed ferret, gray wolf, grizzly bear
Birds—greater prairie chicken, bald eagle, American peregrine falcon, whooping crane
Fish—razorback sucker, humpback chub, Colorado squawfish
Plants—lavender hyssop, spiny-spored quillwort, alpine aster

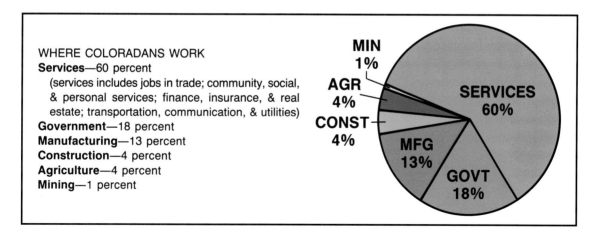

WHERE COLORADANS WORK
Services—60 percent
    (services includes jobs in trade; community, social, & personal services; finance, insurance, & real estate; transportation, communication, & utilities)
Government—18 percent
Manufacturing—13 percent
Construction—4 percent
Agriculture—4 percent
Mining—1 percent

MIN 1%
AGR 4%
CONST 4%
SERVICES 60%
MFG 13%
GOVT 18%

PRONUNCIATION GUIDE

Anasazi (ahn-uh-SAHZ-ee)

Apache (uh-PACH-ee)

Arapaho (uh-RAP-uh-hoh)

Cheyenne (shy-AN)

Comanche (kuh-MAN-chee)

Kiowa (KY-uh-waw)

Mesa Verde (may-suh VEHRD)

Navajo (NAV-uh-hoh)

Pueblo (poo-EHB-loh)

Rio Grande (ree-oh GRAND) or
(ree-oh GRAHN-day)

Santa Fe (sant-uh FAY)

South Platte (SOWTH PLAT)

Ute (YOOT)

Glossary

Anglo A white person of European descent. Anglo is a term used primarily in the Southwest.

bluff A steep, high bank, found especially along a river; a cliff.

colony A territory ruled by a country some distance away.

continental divide A line of elevated land that determines the direction the rivers of a continent flow. In North America, the line is sometimes called the Great Divide. The Rocky Mountains mark the North American divide, separating rivers that flow east from those that flow west.

drought A long period of extreme dryness due to lack of rain or snow.

immigrant A person who moves into a foreign country and settles there.

irrigation A method of watering land by directing water through canals, ditches, pipes, or sprinklers.

Latino A person living in the United States who either came from or has ancestors from Latin America. Latin America includes Mexico and most of Central and South America.

mesa An isolated hill with steep sides and a flat top.

park A flat valley between mountain ranges.

pass A low, passable gap between mountains.

plateau A large, relatively flat area that stands above the surrounding land.

reservation Public land set aside by the government to be used by Native Americans.

smog A heavy haze that forms in the air when smoke and fog combine.

treaty An agreement between two or more groups, usually having to do with peace or trade.

69

Index

Acknowledgments:

Maryland Cartographics, pp. 2, 10; Doyen Salsig, pp. 2–3; Kent & Donna Dannen, pp. 6, 9, 11, 13, 17 (top left & bottom), 18 (inset), 24 (left), 46, 49, 51, 54–55; George Karn, p. 7; Sara Bledsoe, p. 12; R. E. Barber © 1991, p. 14; Karelle Scharff, pp. 15 (left, center, & right), 45, 47, 69; Jerry Hennen, pp. 16, 48 (top right & bottom); Lynda Richards, p. 17 (top right); Museum of Western Colorado, pp. 18 (left) (Al Look Collection, 191.115–775), 34 (right) (Grand Valley Water Users Collection, 1980.115), 36 (Palisade Library Collection, 1972.23–65), 38, (William Chenoweth Collection, 1987.53), 39 (Frank Dean photo, Al Look Collection, 2Ha57e); Starsmore Center for Local History, Colorado Springs Pioneers Museum, pp. 26–27, 63 (bottom left), 64 (top); Colin P. Varga, p. 19; Frederica Georgia, p. 20; All rights reserved, Photo Archives, Denver Museum of Natural History, p. 21; Denver Public Library, Western History Department, pp. 22 (L. Maynard Dixon), 23, 24 (inset), 29 (Arthur Shay), 34 (left), 35 (right), 62 (top right & bottom right), 63 (top left); Colorado Historical Society, pp. 28 (Alex Comparet), 30 (Robert Lindneux), 33 (F1780), 35 (left), 64 (middle) (F8098); Library of Congress, p. 37; C. W. Fentress, J. H. Bradburn and Assoc., Architect, p. 41; Paul A. Pavlik, p. 43; Bob Winsett, Keystone Resort in Colorado, p. 44; Saul Mayer, p. 48 (top left); U.S. Air Force Academy, p. 50; Eric Lars Bakke / Denver Broncos, p. 52; CO Tourism Board, pp. 53 (Jeff Andrew), 61 (Rod Walker); Herbert Fristedt, p. 56; CO Dept. of Health, pp. 57, 59, 65 (bottom right); United Airlines, p. 58; Wisconsin Center for Film and Theater Research, p. 62 (top left); Hollywood Book & Poster Co., p. 62 (center); IPS, pp. 62 (bottom left), 63 (bottom right), p. 64 (bottom), 65 (top left); Hewlett-Packard, p. 63 (top right); NASA, p. 65 (top right); Black American West Museum & Heritage Center, p. 65 (bottom left); Jean Matheny, p. 66; Brown's Royal Gorge Rafting, p. 71.